QUANTUM Book of Songs

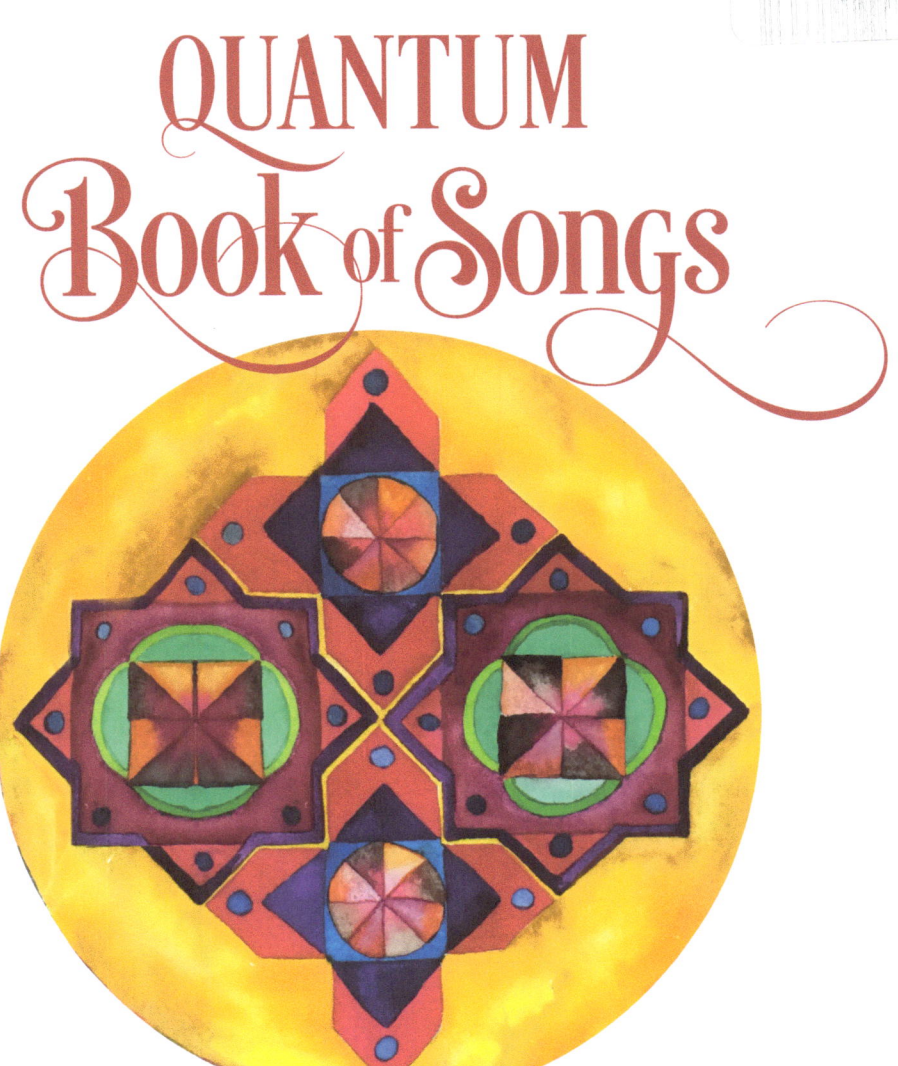

ACCELERATE YOUR TRANSFORMATION WITH HIGH FREQUENCY SONGS OF JOY AND HOPE

JULIE RENEE DOERING

Quantum Book of Songs
Copyright ©2019 by Julie Renee Doering
All rights reserved.

ISBN-13: 978-0-9970044-8-9

Gable-Kennedy Publications All Rights Reserved.
PO Box 549
Carmel Valley, California 93924

Info@Julierenee.com

Printed in the U.S.A.

Book design and cover: Michelle Radomski:
www.onevoicecan.com

No part of this book may be reproduced or transmitted in any form or by any means, electronic or mechanical, including photocopying, recording or by any information storage and retrieval system without written permission of the publisher, except for the inclusion of brief quotations in a review.

Warning – Disclaimer

The purpose of this book is to educate and entertain. The author and/or publisher does not guarantee that anyone following the techniques, suggestions, tips, ideas or strategies will become successful. The author and/or publisher shall have neither liability nor responsibility to anyone with respect to any loss or damage caused, or alleged to be caused, directly by the information in this book.

Endorsement – Disclaimer

Reference herein to any specific commercial products, process, or service by trade name, trademark, manufacturer, or otherwise, in no manner endorses or sponsors the products, processes or offerings.

TABLE OF CONTENTS

A Call to Lighten 2

In Another Time 4

Gather Your Children 6

Love Comes Too Slow 8

The Stones 12

All is Found 16

The Altar 18

The Dream 22

Goodness and Mercy 23

Gentle Night 26

Mystical Temple 28

She Comes to Me 32

Mary's Chapel 36

Sacred Path 38

Speak Softly Gentle Knight 40

Angels and Innocence 42

To The Goddesses of Love, Wisdom, and Divine Protection 46

The Chalice 48

The Mothers Voice 52

Angels Call 54

I Am the Altar 56

Divine Oneness 60

Lakshmi: Love Light Hope! 62

Lady of the Chalice Well 64

In the Stillness 68

About the Singer/Songwriter 70

FOREWORD

Song, especially that of the high frequency variety can move your transformation along at a rapid pace as you move from matching the low mundane frequencies of daily life to the higher frequency of joy, celebration delight and spiritual discovery.

Here for you are the songs I've shared in our on-line trainings for years, favorites like the stones, and a call to lighten, will lift you up and keep you in an elevate place of healing and transformation as you quantum pump your way to a better more fully realized life.

I've been actually writing songs since I was 16 years old. My inner world is a world of song, art and beauty. Many of these songs have been inspired by my spiritual travels whether journeying throughout the globe, or journey through my inner landscape, reflecting my passion for discovering, higher meanings and secrets revealed in the journeying of life.

It is my hope and wish that these songs bring you joy, revelation and awakening as you restore and revitalize all that is you to your fully expressed life of Essence in Body here and now.

With Great Love and Affection

Julie Renee

Your Spiritual Mentor and Guide

A CALL TO LIGHTEN

I wrote this beautiful piece just after the 2001, 9/11 attacks responding to a cry for peace and ease on the planet. During this time, I was holding meditations in my home, it would fill to the brim, literally no room for stepping, as people longed for goodness and to remember the beauty of this world. Imagining a gentle dream, soft the night and sweet the spirit, going to sleep with sweetness and love in the mind heart and body, gentle voices call our song, call out the love and resonance of each as a divine spark. We are magic, we are wonder when we live beyond the veil, the veil of human illusion, beyond the illusion of a reality filled with darkness and evil, we are magic and light. Then asking please humankind, my sisters and brothers, raise the frequency of your consistent thoughts, because thoughts become things, so let us all unite in beautiful thoughts. And as we create the new frequencies of peace and love, the new group mind blessing everyone we can then step into our role as wise elder and guardian spirit incarnate. It comes finally down to the fact that we author this play, this movement of events on the planet. It becomes an urgent need to elevate our actions and our thoughts to truly be the wise guardians of the younger and less mature humans, the inspiration and the mentors of the future.

A CALL TO LIGHTEN

Soft the night and sweet the spirit,
Gentle voices call our song,
We are magic we are wonder
When we live beyond the veil.

Human kind please raise your thoughts
Bring a plane of peace and love
We the guardians of the pilgrims
We the authors of the play.

— 2002 —

IN ANOTHER TIME

After visiting the sites of the King Arthur legends, and seeing the tree where it is said Arthur and Guinevere were laid to rest in the hollow of a huge ancient tree, thinking of all the working aspects of the legend. The Beltane fires, and the fertility rites and passions. The initiation into manhood for Arthur and for the virgin woman priestess who opens up her being to be the goddess of creation. As I was present to the land and mysteries of Avalon I saw and felt the stories play out, the passion, the earthly need to create and the surrender to the will of the goddess directing the seasons of life's genesis.

IN ANOTHER TIME

In another time we laid our bodies down
By wild fires burning our passions roared at Beltane rites
You were a young man
The prince of Camelot
I the virgin priestess
The love of Avalon

We had our moment in time
Our hearts joined as love
We made the kings stage run hard
The goddess knew us as one

You stepped into your manhood
By the goddess initiate
A woman I became
She opened up my gates
This tender moment
we would always treasure
Though times forgotten
this loves great pleasure

GATHER YOUR CHILDREN

It is not well known that I am a good part Irish, and that my great grandmother Katherine Kennedy made her way from Ireland to the US many, many moons ago. She had a loveless marriage in Ireland, ran away to live in love with a good solid man who truly loved her, had four children and then abruptly lost the love of her life. She, a woman of little means, was forced by her mother to give the children away. She gave each of the three girls one by one to people who had shops, could take on another mouth to feed, and they became servants in the homes of these people. The son, who was a babe at the time, she could not part with, and somehow managed to feed and clothe him through the very rough times they lived through. I, too, had the strangeness of deeply loving my three birth children, was an incredibly devoted good mother, but the world had something other in store for these beings and I lost custody of my darlings when they were 5, 3 and 1. I wrote this song knowing the blessings of children and also the pain of loss. I was at the time hoping to bear more children, but was meeting with miscarriage and, again, loss. Children are a blessing, having lost sixteen, three children and thirteen miscarriages, this is my best hopeful and happy advice to mothers. I am now mother to two beautiful children a girl and boy who I love with all my heart.

Build your children up, share with them the secrets and mysteries of life and love give them not only a body and the basics, but give them your heart, your passion your understanding. This way I love you best mothers!

GATHER YOUR CHILDREN

Gather your children oh mommies today
And bind them close to you and love them I pray
And give them your heart your time and your ways

Singing oh bonnie mommies I love you this way,
I love you this way,
I love you this way.

Give them the confidence the care and the play
Talk to them daily about their new world
And share with them light from the mystical planes

Singing oh bonnie mommies I love you this way!
I love you this way,
(*whisper*) I love you this way.

LOVE COMES TOO SLOW

For the lover who never deeply lives into the love relationship with one other, who is always asking, are you my beloved? And for a time, feeling a yes, then fading off once more back in the searching for the beloved, love comes too slow. It comes too slow for the want to be mother who wants children, yet is unable to conceive or carry, this also is the frustration of imagining such beautiful sweet love, yet not realizing it. To actually find love you must be in life, open hearted and ready, you must be seen, and you must be willing to love even if it doesn't lead down your ivory path of Divine partnership. And finally, we must be our own lover first, we must love and welcome our self warmly, accepting all that we are wonderful and not so wonderful, letting go of the stories of imperfection and unlovable and being the embodiment of love, regardless of the past.

LOVE COMES TOO SLOW

Love comes too slow
For those who wait
To find the mystery concealed
Days turn to weeks
And months to years
Still flow the solitary tears

Though every now and then
we glimpse at cupid's hand
And in the magic and
the wonder do we land

Rich flower gardens fill our hearts
With luscious blossoms full expanse
For ever soul to find their mate
We must embark upon the dance

In time, we'll meet love face to face
From life to life
With hope and grace
And if by chance we find that one
Who loves us always as we are

Now take your heart in your own hand
Embrace the gentle lover of the plan
That precious love will find you
where you stand
The love of spirit earth and man

THE STONES

This is an all-time favorite song of both my men and women students. It calls on the power of the stones, grounding and initiating as we clear and regenerate. I wrote this song after several wonderful spiritual pilgrimages and a period of study with the Native Americans in Wind Tree temple Santa Cruz Mountains. What I was mystically feeling into was how present the stones are, and how their energies are ready to help heal and soothe the peoples of the earth. You need not be with the particular stone to enjoy its masterful energies and healing qualities. I was strongly drawn to the ancient stone temples of initiation, and enjoyed visions of the activities from the olden times as I allowed myself to feel and be fully present to the blessings of the powerfully magical ruins. I had the great fortune of doing ceremony inside the circle of Stonehenge, at summer solstice, beings of light above us initiating us while an Angelic Female spirit with ribbons of pink and gold lead the joyous celebration. Avebury felt ancient and sexual, there was a great deal of pleasure, ecstasy and laughter, as the stones invited us to lay down and enjoy the moment. New Grange stones, ancient stone temples underground, held mystery and revelation. As I placed my head on the basin stone, images of ceremony and life 4000 years ago played out in my inner vision. Spirals of time, helping the transition on and off the planet. And finally, the medicine wheel and the reminder of creating sacredness where ever we go simply by aligning stones as if to create an alter and sacred space, placing rocks in a circle and crossing this circle with additional stones in a reverent way.

THE STONES

Chorus:
The stones they are a calling me
Echoing through an eternity
Calling out to set us free
The power of the stones

At dawn, I walked in a circle of stones
A solar temple to me yet unknown
Till by the strength of first mornings light
Shown the power of the Stonehenge stones

They grounded the energy of this place
And held us together in loving embrace
While beings of light danced above the space
Bestowing on us their wisdom and grace

Chorus

The Avebury stones were laughing at me
Taunting me tempting me dancing with glee
Playful stones make love to me
In the circle of the stones

Chorus

The heavenly chambers from days of old
New Grange stones were a circle to behold
I knelt in prayerful reverence
For the power of the basin stone

I touched my forehead to the rock
It filled me with bright light and talk
Of the ancient people and their ways
And the spirals of the stones

Chorus

Stones are everywhere we look
Medicine wheels and monolithic books
The wisdom of the circle flows
In the temple of the stones

Chorus

— 2002 —

ALL IS FOUND

This song has a profound and deep feeling of coming out of a horrific time, and emerging back to the light rapidly with trust and hope. I had gone through a time of illness and as I was pulling myself out of that health crisis, I also left a fiancé, moved into a little bungalow and began life again single. But not long after this two unthinkable things happened. I was given a date rape drug on Thanksgiving Day, brutally raped and left in terrible condition. Just as I was starting to come back into my body and begin to heal, I was run over by a car, bled out through a head injury lying on the road, with no pulse or blood pressure when ambulance arrived. I had angelic helpers with me, and a long 5-year recovery process began in a wheel chair with a bad traumatic brain injury. All is Found, speaks of the worst of human condition, and the perfection and love that allows for a rapid shift back to the light. This is such a helpful song as we let go of the past, let go of identifying with the traumas of our life and allow the trust and grace to reappear.

ALL IS FOUND

Just when I think that all is lost
And there's nothing more than I can do
When the pain in my heart gets to great
And I feel that I will explode

When all is lost and hope is nowhere
When I find myself screaming in terror
I find my depth, my center, my light
While surrendering to my essence

Grace finds a way to melt away the tears
And a soothing gentle trust reappears

When all is calm and I find myself at one
When chaos is transformed into clarity
Grace finds a way to melt away the tears
And a soothing gentle trust reappears

THE ALTAR

This is a recounting of a very magical cross time celebration. The Abbey of Joseph is a reference to the ruins of the cathedral in Glastonbury, England, where it is said Joseph of Arimathea, Jesus' uncle, traveled to and set up a small monastery after the crucifixion. Love and high frequency energy were in the air. I was warmly welcomed by a reverent man, Paul Weston, a Mystic, who was happy to come along on this magical day for delights across time. I felt pulled to the Mary chapel that had been slightly restored with a lovely new altar, amidst the ruins of the church. As I chanted and called forth an awakening of light, Paul lifted me up and sat me on this altar. My experience was other worldly, and simply glorious. As I continued to pray the ancient gnostic prayers, the chapel ruins lit with a spiritual light. I felt light flowing through me, and the parade of my goddess forms from previous incarnations played through my body, as color, light, and frequency danced all around me, and through the chapel. Ecstatic and blissful, a moment in time to remember with great joy.

THE ALTAR

It happened one day in the Abbey of Joseph
It happened one day in the magic of love
It happened one day
I was filled with the spirit
Of the mother who comes from above

I saw her standing behind me
The black Madonna was she
And before me I saw the Christ of my childhood
My friend of eternity

I looked round the nave
It was brilliant with spirit
Four bridesmaids attended me
My body the altar
Full of light flowing freely
The goddess enchanted be

The flame burned so brightly
The canopy covered
The altar so sacred divine
I was the bride and the priestess of this day
My bridegroom the logos of time

My gown was effulgent
My spirit was soaring
And I was a spirit set free
The wonder of mystical union communion
Was the dancing of a peaceful sea

I spoke with my voice
It was clear bright and vibrant
The song of my heart echoing
I let go of fear to the love of the goddess
And the joy of infinity

THE DREAM

This is a dream about divine love longing for fulfillment. In this song I was privileged to enjoy being the witness to this kind of magical love. As if in another reality, the experience of breathing them in, hearing their whispers, touching their presence, being comforted and nurtured by this beautiful embracing dream. Waking to the knowledge that I am loved, included, and cared for as we all are in the realms where Divine beings make their home.

THE DREAM

I saw him the author of dreams
I heard him whispering sweet things
I felt him the loneliest of beings
I breathed him like fresh mountain air

I saw her the goddess complete
I touched her and found myself at peace
I hungered and she was there to feed me
I wearied embraced by holy hand

He loved her like bees to a flower
She loved him and out of love came power
I saw him heard him felt him
I breathed her touched and embraced her

GOODNESS AND MERCY

This psalm written and sung by King David affirms, no matter what, I am blessed, and that I shall live in the house of the Lord, the house of love and Divine righteousness forever. It is a strong affirmation that life is always working and we are always blessed no matter how things appear. And that by affirming this often we rise above the mundane with complete confidence and trust. All that I want, all I'll ever be expands from this affirmation... flows into the most exquisite beautiful life I could hope for. The repetition of these powerful words like a mantra create a set point and foundation for all of life, and the expectation followed by the creation of wonder, love and blessing.

GOODNESS AND MERCY

Surely goodness and mercy shall follow me all the days of my life
And I shall dwell in the house of the lord, for ever and ever amen

All that I am and all that I can be is expanding from this mystery

Surely goodness and mercy shall follow me all the days of my life
And I shall dwell in the house of the lord, for ever and ever amen

All that I want and all I'll ever be is flowing from this loving seed

Surely goodness and mercy shall follow me all the days of my life
And I shall dwell in the house of the lord, for ever and ever amen

— September 2003 —

GENTLE NIGHT

The sweetness of the pitter patter of raindrops like a baptism of new life washing away the sorrows and pains of life. Having struggled with the meaning and purpose of my life and depression with anxiety and panic, knowing it was not me, but not knowing how to resolve it, I was, at this time, in the search for both meaning and a steadfast movement to a life filled with grace and ease. This verse acknowledges the oneness with God, who is the God of peace and gentleness. And though I teach not to match another, in this case matching the peace and grace of the Divine can be a tremendous uplifting of spirit and a profound healing to body as both drop into the parasympathetic system of rest and recovery.

GENTLE NIGHT

Gentle night rain falling softly
Gentle night soft falls the rain
We are one, one with the raindrops,
we are one with the god of rain

Gentle night cleansing my spirit
Soft falling rain drops
Wash away my tears
All is well in the house of the raindrops
All is well in the garden of love

— 2004 —

MYSTICAL TEMPLE

The joy of stepping into holy places, energized by worship and ritual, filled with angels and connection with God is the theme of this wonderful song. Mystical temple is a familiar reference to the cathedrals churches and temples I've enjoyed and worshiped in. Each holy place was designed with sacred geometry in mind, so both beautiful and magnificent in structure and energy. Visons of splendor and happy reunions speaks to the ecstatic joy of coming into the presence of Jesus Christ, Mother Mary, Father Mother God, and Angels, feeling hopeful and aware, present to the awe and wonder this world offers. Joy, pleasure, a spirit filled with light and happiness. Dancing and singing to the fullness and expansion of the original pranic breath! Held by mother earth and embraced by father sky, the cathedral, a complete parent, the nave, its belly or sacred womb. Nurturing the seekers, the children of light.

MYSTICAL TEMPLE

Oh, mystical temple I sing to your glory
The sacred geometry folds echoing sounds
Oh, visions of splendor and happy reunions
Through eras and friendships that vibrate through time

I sing in your vibrancy, dancing of spirit
I sing in the echo that prances through time
And holding back nothing my voice raised in splendor
Ecstatically chanting my voice merged with all

Majestic your chapel oh holy cathedral
I bow with the reverence of energy divine
Earth mother holds you and sky father blesses you
And I laugh in the pleasures of reverberating sound

Oh, church in your structure I see you the mother
The body of spirit the goddess in your form
Oh, sacred sweet sanctuary a safe and a warm womb
Embracing our spirits in embryonic form

From age to ages I've sang in your belly
I've cried in my sorrows and rejoiced in the love
For the memories of spirit are easily remembered
In the place where the mother nurtures her child.

— 2003 —

SHE COMES TO ME
IN HONOR OF MOTHER MARY

In my striving to heal my heart, having been born to a physically beautiful, but mentally challenge mother, my need to have a bond with a mother figure so clearly became letting go of the earthly mother for Divine Mother Mary. This song speaks to the suffering of humankind and the love of Mary, and of course many other divine female beings who love and care for us, who serve humanity endlessly, helping ease the suffering, uplift the spirit of so many, and restore hope.

SHE COMES TO ME
IN HONOR OF MOTHER MARY

She comes to me,
In early morning
When all is quiet *(repeat 3 times)*

Before the birds
Have awakened,
To sing their sweet song *(repeat 3 times)*

There she is
My Holy Mother
Giving me comfort,
Giving me sweet rest.

I long to be with her,
To serve her in spirit
Long to take refuge
from this human form.

Who cares for us,
When ones of us are struggling?
When life feels so desperate *(repeat 3 times)*

Who cares
For the broken hearted?
Who cares for my soul? *(repeat 1 time)*
When all is quiet,
She sings her sweet song.
When life seems so desperate,
She cares for my soul.

— 2003 —

MARY'S CHAPEL

Having been raised Lutheran the adoration of Mary was frowned upon, yet I did find my way to her comforting presence in my mid to late twenties; greatly in need of a divine feminine spiritual refuge. I had been a singer. I sang solos everywhere in my youth and early marriage. I sang in a professional choir, major works, I thought of myself that way. When cancer surgery paralyzed my vocal chords, I didn't know how I could live. Without song, who was I? Years down the road, kneeling in prayer at the Basilica of St. Mary's, she came to me, standing 12 feet in front of me, she asked me to sing. I said I could not, and she raised her hand in invitation to sing, and I did. The voice that came out of me was surprising, I sounded like and angel, even to myself. I felt strong and sure, singing in Latin, raising my voice in great joy, as a chorus of what sounded like 1000 angels filled the cathedral with a sustained and glorious ahhhhh. My vocal cords had not healed, I could just now sing. And now with the quantum work, my vocal cords are completely restored, and better than ever. I am so grateful for her presence, love and encouragement.

MARY'S CHAPEL

There is a softness about her
Sweet mother Mary
I can only respond to her in love

There is a reverence surrounding her
Precious Mother Mary
I can only respond to her in awe

There is such a holiness *(repeat 3 times)*
Pure precious holiness

My hearts filled with ecstasy *(repeat 3 times)*
With Mother Mary as my guide

SACRED PATH

The sacred path refers to the labyrinth, a walking meditation found in many cathedrals. I have walked the sacred path on both labyrinths at Grace Cathedral many times. The art of walking meditation is simple. Begin with a prayer, and a reverent feeling. Know that this walk will give you what you seek and surrender prayerfully to the path ahead. As the labyrinth takes you to both the farthest points away from the center and back again close to the core, you may notice the familiarity with the flow of life. Sometimes feeling very close to your divine self and oneness while other times, perhaps slogging through the mundane, getting the stuff of life done. All of it is the fulfillment of life. As you reach the center you may feel a subtle awareness and an awakening to the answer you had hoped to glean, or it may surface in the coming days. Resting in the center, like returning to the spiritual womb of Divine mother, for nourishment and rest than leaving out the birth canal back into life, the path out feels like a sacred reentry time, slow and gentle, allowing for peaceful grace and ease to move you back to your life nourished, uplifted and wiser for having walked the path.

SACRED PATH

Your sacred path leads me
To the womb of the mother
And walking with reverence
My soul path to discover
On days when I weary
My heart encumbered
I looked to the labyrinth
To revive and uncover

Oh, sacred path the journey for life
Let my steps with the spirit be one
The love is brilliant
On the path to the mother
And when we're restored
We bring forth the light
Peace and center
Our calm and surrender

— 2002 —

SPEAK SOFTLY GENTLE KNIGHT

Written after a wonderful adventure in the land of King Arthur and his knights, and a wonderful experience of chivalry. It was June in England. I had dressed for a summer day, gotten in a tour van carrying about fifteen of us, a couple hours from Glastonbury to Tintagel, the original site of King Arthur's castle ruins. We made our way down to Merlin's cave, down a cliff face and into a cave on the beach. As we imagined Merlin's magic and watched as visions moved across the ceiling of the cave, the tides came in and the cave floor was flooded and about twelve inches of cold ocean water was now in front of us to walk through. I was very surprised about the brisk weather, it must have been about 45 degrees, the ocean winds had come up, and an icy rain was falling in sheets. I scaled the cliff face back towards civilization and ducked into a kiosk where trinkets of King Arthur and his knights were being sold. There a kind man dressed as a knight was behind the counter selling his wares, and talking of the divine feminine. Seeing me shaking like a leaf, chilled to the bone, he came out from the counter and held me till I was warm once more. A moment in time I will always remember, true gentle chivalry.

SPEAK SOFTLY GENTLE KNIGHT

Speak softly gentle knight
Your kindness to reveal
Hold me in your strong arms
And warm my frozen heart

Tell me of legends old
Of Arthur and his bride
Bring stories back to life
Your gentleness exposed

Speak softly gentle knight
Of honor code and rule
The ways of chivalry
Bring to this century

And when I smile at you
Your eyes alight with mine
Your costume and your ways
Speak true of Gelfad days

ANGELS AND INNOCENCE

I start this song with the longing for, and honoring of, innocence and the divine connection we have to angels. This day I was feeling the amalgamation of the good and bad done by powers in the catholic church. Perhaps struggling to want it all to be aligned with the teaching and pure truth Christ Jesus brought for us, and not being so naive to see that a few "Bishops and Holy One" were responsible for a good deal of pain suffering and disorder. Maybe not all are meant to be part of this level of purity and truth. I know that I can be knocked over (kicked out of my own church as a young woman leaving her husband) shunned, and yet I do get back up, I stand once more in the light and connection of love with God. Coming to the idea, okay, this higher frequency is not the big picture even for some who promote the business of Christ and salvation and knowing I am well even if this is true.

ANGELS AND INNOCENCE

Angels and Innocence
Time racing by
Babies and mothers
Hope in their eyes

Saintly and sovereignly
Soft spoken love
Bishops and holy ones
Moving their pawns

Play with the universe
Alter the plan
Stop making victims
Love is at hand

Honest and open
Hearts flowing free
Find me a spirit
Truthful to me

Life is a mystery
Passions a chance
Not all are meant to be
Part of this dance

Knock me right over
I'll stand up again
I am the mystery
Of loves great depth

TO THE GODDESSES OF LOVE, WISDOM AND DIVINE PROTECTION

Having lived in India and returned in this incarnation at age 33 to remember what I had known and accomplished in other lifetimes, The three goddesses that are the pillars of the Divine Feminine in Hinduism, playful, wise, loving, and filled with grace, are good to remember and call upon their names frequently.

Lakshmi is considered the goddess of love, she also is the goddess of the home, wealth, and beauty. Sarasvati is the goddess of wisdom, the arts, and sciences. She is lovely, with a round face and kind demeanor. Durgama rides on the back of a white tiger, beautiful, and devoted to her children, a fierce protector energy comes when invoking her name. The tradition in India is to often chant the names of the gods and goddesses, I look at these as powerful spirit guides, helpers, and advocates, and that if you have your mind turned to them, you will at the time of death, pass right to the highest heaven. It is a lovely notion.

TO THE GODDESSES OF LOVE, WISDOM AND DIVINE PROTECTION

Lakshmi goddess, beauty grace and heart
Abundant love shining through
You the light of a loving graceful maker
Lakshmi goddess of my heart

Sarasvati goddess of my passion
Song and art and wisdom shining through
Guide my thoughts in the music of the ether
And calm the waters of my soul

Durgama, Mother fierce protector
Protect me from my woos
Break the bonds of egos earthly enchantments
Restore me to my whole

— 2011 —

THE CHALICE

This is a meandering tale about the chalice said to have been used in the last supper by Lord Jesus with his disciplines. The story tells itself, but I'll share with you my time with the chalice. About 20 years ago, I was introduced to the chalice well gardens. At that time, my new friend Paul Weston had mentioned to me several times he felt I should be with the "blue bowl." This was a mysterious code, what was the blue bowl I wondered? And I found out it was said to be a 3400-year-old glass bowl formed in Egypt, used for sacred ceremony, and had, after the crucifixion of Christ, been brought up to England, with a small amount of Jesus Christ's blood and sweat. Perhaps, it is thought, Joseph of Arimathea had carried it up with him as a power piece and a presence when he started his monastery. I returned a year later, and having fully comprehended what was suggested, I went to the keepers of the chalice to ask permission to sit with the bowl. It had been well kept, and was hidden, not being used for ceremony, resting. As the keeper asked the bowl, the answer was yes. This surprised everyone as it had been hidden for many months allowing no one to touch it. I was given a 45-minute window to hold the bowl, meditate with it and enjoy the connection with this very special and sacred vessel.

THE CHALICE

Three thousand years ago,
An alchemist did bind
A symbol of the cross
In a chalice blue and fine

A splendid work of art
Came out of Egypt land
Destined for sacredness
Embraced by holy hand

And power was its fate
God's vessel in the land
For all of Human kind
To share this blessing sublime

Through ages it was kept
And preciously retained
And used for holy works
The chalice found its way

The one we know as Christ
Caressed this sacred bowl
And drank from it the wine
He shared his blood with all

And on the cross, he hung
And sweat and blood did flow
Into this holy grail
God's physical presence flowed

Within a year or two
The chalice left Israel's lands
And to Great Britain soil
In brother Joseph's hands

The sanctuary he built
The chalice a symbol of hope
But ages past again
Man plundered our treasured cup

And power was its fate
God's vessel in the land
For all of Human kind
To share this blessing sublime

Lost it did remain
For centuries to come
Away from harmful hands
Embraced by mother earth

And blessed was the land
And rich her earthly soil
Blossoms of love did sprout
To bless all human kind

Safely through the raging storms
Of human history
The chalice did survive
in Somerset County

Oh, Mystic Avalon
Revealed this cup to girls
They sacredly revered
This precious Holy Grail

Now women guard the cup
And use it prayerfully
To heal this weary earth
And restore our human family

And power was its fate
God's vessel in the land
For all of Human kind
To share this blessing sublime

THE MOTHER'S VOICE

In the exploration of the feminine the sacred and profane, I explore the ancient wisdom of the mother and her tenuous relationship with mankind. I refer to an ancient concept that the goddess of wisdom gives herself to the depths of matter to protect the light of spirit by becoming the soul, the holder of all human light. And of course, the invitation she always graciously extends to her children, walk with me precious, I am your mother, I hold your light, I love you.

THE MOTHER'S VOICE

I have been
And will continue
I am the ancient of your womanhood
Mankind has honored me
Mankind has scorned me
Yet I continue
Continue to be

Hold to me tightly
Reach for me always
I will protect and preserve your sweet soul
For I am the vessel
I am the chalice
I hold the spark and the light burning in you

Walk with me precious
I am the mothers voice
I am the sanctity
I am pure love.

ANGELS CALL

This celebrates the loving connection between humans and angels and was written after a dream where I saw and felt the role of angels as helpers and guardians. Since writing this wonderful and very sweet piece I have done a great deal of research on angels and have found our connections with those who align with humanity to be profound, loving offering protection and care. In a black and white world where angels seem to be a simple fantasy, we can awaken to the world of wonder and know we are never alone.

ANGELS CALL

Angels call while we are sleeping
Riding through the waves of dreams
Keeping safe our mortal bodies
While we play in astral scenes

Beams of light flow from their bodies
Showing us a glimmering mirror
Waking to the world of wonder
Leaves behind all doubt and fear

— 2003 —

I AM THE ALTAR

If you are everything, if you acknowledge there is nothing you are not, a broad and deep knowing for life, with not just one view or one vision of life, but seeing things from 100 unique perspectives can begin to reveal itself, and wise elder wisdom becomes the new set point. We are the innocent, and we are the ones who are in the wrong at times, saying this, knowing it to be true, welcomes growth, removes blame, and assigning responsibility to another, and ultimately gives you full power over your life. The beauty in this song is to imagine being all that is sacred, and perfect in a mystical ceremony, and then being that which is worship also, being one with the great I am. Then, Sophia, goddess of wisdom, said to be the soul, the darkness, the word incarnate, the logo and the delight associated with the union of logos with Sophia, goddess of wisdom. To be weak and yet strong, this piece invites opposites to be as one, and the singer to be liberated in the field of oneness.

I AM THE ALTAR

I am the altar
I am the lamb
I am receptive
I am I am

I am Sophia
I am dark night
I am the logos
I am delight

I am communion
Body and Blood
I am forgiveness
I am the love

I am the mother
I am the son
I am the father
I am as one

I am the incense
Fragrant desire
I am the ashes
Burnt by the fire

I am the innocent
I am the wrong
I am the delicate
I am the strong

DIVINE ONENESS

This is a reminder that there is great plenty and constant help if we all but ask. Think about the nurturing and loving fruits of spirit, and divine connection. What comes from God is fulfilling and magnificent sweetness we can't even imagine. Imagine the Divine, mother father God as a parent who loves us beyond measure, who supports our free will, but longs to shower us with everything wonderful we can imagine will make our life amazing. Imagine as you chant these words you are being filled with the light of God, you are the recipient of this greatest love and greatest out pouring of spiritual gifts. Wonder! Joy! Home! Love! Fulfillment of Purpose!

DIVINE ONENESS

Come to me all you who yearn for me
And be filled with my fruits.

You will remember me
As sweeter than honey

LAKSHMI: LOVE LIGHT HOPE!

TO THE GODDESS OF BEAUTY, GRACE, LOVE, AND WEALTH

Lakshmi, beautiful independent woman/goddess, owned by no god, standing on her own with the greatest power to transform and create that a female can wield. There is a legend of Lakshmi; both human and demon races found themselves in great need of help. They stopped their warring and together churned the sea with prayer and chanting till many things emerged, and finally the goddess Lakshmi who could save the earth. She handles well both darkness and light, though is radiantly beautiful and light herself. In other sweet traditions Lakshmi is a kind of Santa Claus, delivering gifts to good little children on her special night.

LAKSHMI: LOVE LIGHT HOPE!

TO THE GODDESS OF BEAUTY, GRACE, LOVE, AND WEALTH

Be my guide in dark times
Be my guide in light times

Be my light in dark times
Be my light in light times

Be my love in dark times
Be my love in light times

Be my hope in dark times
Be my hope in light times

Be my help in dark times
Be my help in light times

Be my wealth in dark times
Be my wealth in light times

— 2009 —

LADY OF THE CHALICE WELL

On my first trip to the chalice well gardens I had the pleasure of experiencing a beautiful guardian spirit rise up from the well and greet me. She was lovely gracious and clearly there as an initiator. As I interacted with her, she showed me in an inner vision my own hesitation of stepping into really owning my priesthood, of stepping into the Divine Blessing I came to share with the world. The invitation was just that, I could choose what I wanted and when. I see that this moment was one of many that lead to my awakening and remembering of who I am, and the meaning of my life, why I had suffered and struggled so much, and what I know to do in the way I do it in the world.

LADY OF THE CHALICE WELL

Oh, lady of the chalice well
Your grace doth mystify my soul
The guardian spirit of the sacred well
And keeper of the holy grail

I am enchanted by your priestess veil
And honored by your light
You grace us with your spirit so sublime
And bless us with your care divine

The songs we sing
That pass-through time
Do bring you forth
For us to know

Invoking you to shine your truth
Illuminate all seekers here

Oh, precious moment
When first we met
A brilliant star did shine
And from this place
Above the chalice well
Emerged through webs of time

You spoke to me
It was my time
To be the priestess told
I spoke my fears
You said you understood
But what was I to choose?

Lady of the chalice well
Life restored,
Free from fear,
Living well
And I entranced,
My spirit danced
With bright and joyful flow.

I heard these words
I felt I must comply
You answered softly
no
The choice is mine
I must choose with freewill
To make the priesthood mine

The help is here,
It's all around me now
And I am not alone
She gave me back
What had been lost to me
The honor of free will

I surrendered to the fear
I surrendered to the hope
I am willing to be
My destiny unfold

Lady of the chalice well
Treats us all so very well
Bringing the sisterhood
A power source
Inspiring human spirits
On their sacred path

IN THE STILLNESS

This is the song of spirit, essence, and the flow of Essence in life. Becoming aware of more, of stillness and quiet, of an open heart filled with love, this is where the divine spark of each of us can be found. I am essence, the fullness of all parts of spirit, including sacred Pranic breath, light divine I am I am. I claim this is who I am. I affirm this power, and I awaken to this presence of God, self-alive in me. Perfect used as a chant, invocation and as a completion song of sacred coming together.

IN THE STILLNESS

In the stillness
In the quiet
In the open heart
There I am

I am essence
I am breath
I am light of God
I am I am

— 2003 —

ABOUT THE SINGER/SONGWRITER

Julie Renee refuses to play small. She powerfully mentors those who are being taken out of the game with exhaustion and "fuzzy brain." She regenerates the brain and gets them back to playing at 100% again.

Books by Julie Renee include: *Your Divine Human Blueprint, Quantum Healing Secrets, 100% You Formula, Breakthrough, Balance Your Life Now,* and *Illumination.*

Julie Renee is the founder and developer of a new spiritual science, the 100% Healthy Human Blueprint. She is the author of the ground-breaking book, *Your Divine Human Blueprint.* Her unique gift of healing defines the energy-science of Cellular Quantum Mechanics. She trains individuals in her "100% You Immersion Program" and sees private VIP clients in her home in northern California.

After launching her first business from her tiny San Francisco studio apartment in 1993, she has prevailed over a challenging history of multiple cancers and five near-death experiences. Overcoming tremendous odds, none of her doctors saw a possibility for her to survive her illnesses; she was repeatedly told she was dying. Unwilling to believe that this was true, even the Angel of Death could not convince her that it was her time to go. She has dedicated her life to the

betterment of humankind and the reawakening of humanity to the Divine Human Blueprint.

Recognized for her leadership abilities, she is the recipient of the 2010-2011 National Association of Professional Women's "Woman of the Year Award" and the Powerful Women International's "Global Leadership Award" 2012.

Julie Renee has been featured as an expert on CBS, Unity FM, Rock Star Radio, Blog Talk Align, Live 365, Low Down, *Spirit Seeker, 11: 11 Magazine, Spirit Seeker Magazine,* and on various TV shows, including "New Era Healing" and a "Forum on Spirituality." She is a writer for *Holistic Fashionista Magazine* and *Accomplish Magazine.* She is also the host of the radio show, *100% Healthy.* Additionally, she has both stage and film credits, and is a harpist and singer.

Julie Renee is *the* 100% Healthy Life EXPERT. She is the founder and Mentor for the Quantum Activations Academy, presenting trainings to a global student following, mentoring and certifying hundreds of students each year in her unique trainings on the Divine human blueprint, Cellular Neo Genesis and profound clearings in all aspects of life.

From Farm Wife to Health Activator

Julie Renee started out in Minnesota as a farm wife, attended art school, modeled, waitressed, appeared in seven films, became a very successful realtor, and finally moved into her passion as a healer in the form of a health activator. She now has over thirty years' experience supporting individuals and groups in Quantum Health Activations, from high-risk pregnancies to life-saving interventions with critically ill individuals. Known as the premier healer for high risk pregnancies, twenty doctors and six midwives sent their most difficult clients to Julie Renee to help them from gestation through the first year after birth. In all, she has assisted more than one hundred and forty high risk babies to successfully enter this world.

Many years ago, she taught yoga and offered healing massage to people in recovery. She also taught infant massage, worked with insurance companies, and helped injured clients return to living, and hospice clients pass from this world, pain-free and without medication as they said good-by to their loved ones.

Moving deeper into her exploration of regeneration, she developed specialized Jadeite hot stone treatments, accessing the knowledge of the ancient civilizations of the Olmecs and Mayans, who used Jadeite for body initiations and transformations.

As part of a natural progression, Julie Renee moved from physical healing to offering spiritual life coaching for women. Through her clairvoyant gifts, she helped women rapidly shift to move into their next highest step.

For the past eleven years, Julie Renee has been researching and developing programs with the Blueprint, teaching through guidebooks, courses and

meditation as a simple way to access the healing gifts and secrets of the Divine Human Blueprint.

Thousands of individuals have created health, wealth and love with Julie Renee's help. Through her extraordinary gifts, she has brought critically ill people back into their lives, restoring health to their cellular and energetic bodies through the Divine Human Blueprint.

Traveling the world, she has studied in India, and is both an ordained minister and a pujari (carrier of the light) in the yogic tradition.

Julie Renee's favorite vacations include rappelling down waterfalls, zip lining, and performing daring acts, such as shooting down the longest water slide in Mexico. She loves the ocean, the mountains, and nature, and is a nature girl at heart. You can find her out hiking trails every chance she gets. She challenges herself regularly by rappelling, and doing other fun but scary activities that involve hanging from great heights with ropes. Her favorite ice cream is rose petal. She loves mangos and scented flowers, especially garden roses.

Julie Renee can be reached through her website at:

www.JulieRenee.com

or on any of the following social sites: Facebook, YouTube, LinkedIn, and Twitter.

www.ingramcontent.com/pod-product-compliance
Lightning Source LLC
Chambersburg PA
CBHW060819090426
42738CB00002B/37